SKYSCRAPERS-
SKYPRICKERS-
SKYCITIES

SKYSCRAPERS-SKYPRICKERS-SKYCITIES

Charles Jencks

Academy Editions

In memory of Betty Houston

Acknowledgements: This photo-essay on the tall building has been immensely helped by different people who are cited in the footnotes or photographic credits. Most of the slides are my own, but a few are those of friends and professional photographers who have kindly responded to fill obvious gaps. There are, inevitably, many significant buildings which are not illustrated here, but I have tried to give the most heterogeneous possible selection. Maggie Keswick has once again provided editorial advice and some sharp suggestions from which I have benefited, and I am also particularly grateful to Rem Koolhaas who has commented on the text and lent me important books. His *Delirious New York*, the investigation of the content and motives behind tall buildings, sets a standard for other skyscrapologists to reach, and one from which I have learned much even if I have not followed its direction. My study is limited to the form and expression of the tall building, but those interested in the unexpurgated version might consult his work of supreme fiction both for its insight and wit.

Front Cover
PHILIP JOHNSON and JOHN BURGEE, *I.D.S. Center*, Minneapolis, Minnesota, 1972-5.

Back cover
San Francisco, 1972, varieties of skyscrapers, skyprickers and skycities.

First published in Great Britain in 1980 by
Academy Editions, 7/8 Holland Street, London W8

ISBN: 85670-679-5

Printed and bound in Hong Kong

CONTENTS

Figures refer to illustration numbers

INTRODUCTION

The history of the skyscraper has, in the past, proven hard to write – and even harder to think about. The more that historians and scholars grapple with this voluminous subject the more elusive it becomes, disappearing into the mists of uncharted territory and contradictory definition. One finally concludes in exasperation that the history of the skyscraper is an impossible subject to clarify because it doesn't exist. And yet there is the evidence before our eyes in every large city, and the testimony of the public who have a very clear idea of what a skyscraper is: the Empire State Building, or the Chrysler Building, and now, the largest building in the world, the Sears Tower in Chicago. They all touch the sky in a way which could be loosely called 'scraping'. The French naturally have a precise idea of this building type too, indicated in their reverberant appellation *gratte-ciel*. One can hear in the rolling r's – grrrratte – a very aggressive sound, as if the tall building were really scraping off the undersides of passing clouds. The Spanish *rascacielos* ('scratch-sky') shreds up the clouds while the German *wolkenkratzers* ('cloud-scratchers') cracks them up. (A Russian designer proposed flat 'skyhooks' which the Germans called 'cloudirons' because they smoothed off the bottoms of cumulous clouds.) Almost every language has adopted the word and notion of the skyscraper, which was first put into circulation in New York during the 1880s. How can its history not exist?

The problem is one of definition, or the lack of it. Architectural historians have taken a limited view of the subject, both in time and substance. They confine their attention to the last hundred years and carefully overlook the most difficult and interesting aspect of the building type – its expressive quality. Thus many of their tall buildings don't scrape at all, but sit horizontally and four-square on the ground, or rise hesitantly in tiers like a stepped wedding cake. They might be large 'skylumps', or 'skycakes', or 'skysquatters' or 'skypalaces', but they are not often sky*scrapers*. Moreover so many vertical, pointing towers should really be reclassified as 'skyneedles', 'skypins' or the general category 'skyprickers'. The whole subject of tall buildings has to be rethought from the beginning.

A typical historian's definition is the following: 'Skyscraper. A *multi-storey* building constructed on a *steel skeleton*, provided with high-speed electric *elevators* and combining extraordinary *height* with ordinary room spaces such as would be used in low buildings.'[1] (My italics.) This four-part definition (if we subtract the definer 'ordinary room space') is shared by most historians. Winston Wiseman, the dean of skyscrapologists, reiterates the orthodox agreement on this subject in his recent 'A New View of Skyscraper History'.[2] With the definition thus agreed, a debate then ensues on the question of the first skyscraper. One historian holds that it is the Masonic Temple Building, 1891-2, because it has 20 usable storeys, a height of 300 feet, skeletal structure and elevators (actually it *looks* like a squat skypalace); another historian favours the Home Life Insurance Company Building, 1884-5, which has the same elements in only 10 storeys (and this, with its horizontal expression, looks like a skycage). In fact Wiseman, after much thought and reconsideration of the data, pushes back the date.

> After much contemplation, I would like to change my earlier position. My vote for the 'first skyscraper' goes to the Equitable Life Assurance Company Building raised in New York during 1868-70 by Gilman and Kendall and George B. Post (i). The reasons: the Equitable was the first *business* building in which the possibilities of the *elevator* were realized. It rose to a *height* of 130 feet, which made it twice as tall as the average five storey commercial building.[3] (My emphasis.)

Wiseman does not say whether this building has a metal skeleton (it does) and he is still not clear over the necessity for this as part of his definition (does it rule out reinforced concrete?). A more important lacuna is, however, the expressive part: the Equitable is horizontal, flat, squat, a Renaissance palazzo with a mansard roof and not 'a proud and soaring thing' in Louis Sullivan's panegyric to the tall building. How can the first skyscraper not scrape? Because, if one explores Wiseman further, this building proved that the elevator worked safely and efficiently, it was a financial success and it led to other business buildings. Thus the function and pragmatism of the building type are assuming a place in the definition of the skyscraper: it must be a place of business and corporate pride, as well as having the other four qualities.

But this compound definition still has its problems: it again leaves out expressiveness and it limits the function to business or commerce. It is true that most tall buildings are built by large corporations intent on signifying their worth, but some are residences, schools and landmark towers. Are these not skyscrapers? Is the Lake Point Tower, a 70 storey residential tower, removed from consideration because of its function (26)? And what of more contentious towers, Eiffel's in Paris or Kikutake's in Osaka, or the one in Brugge finished in the 15th century, 250 feet high, the equivalent of a 25 storey building? It's a strange definition which can expand and contract at will, sometimes

i The Historians' first skyscraper: GILMAN & KENDALL and GEORGE B. POST, *The Equitable Life Assurance Company Building*, New York, 1868-70.

making elevators necessary, other times making business, structure, height and motivation necessary, and at no time making expression necessary. It is necessary to start again with a compound definition which reflects the complexity of the facts. The first tall building that 'scraped' the sky was not built in New York in 1868, and a more accurate history will take us back much further in time – to the first obelisks, ziggurats and pyramids built 3,000 years ago, or to heaven-aspiring structures built before that. Man has been constructing skybuildings for a long time and skyscraper architects, aware of this tradition, have incorporated its morphology and metaphors into their own creations to the point where it becomes arbitrary and obscure to insist on a restricted definition. Skyscrapers are part of a much larger set of skybuildings.

Morphology + articulation + style + activity + technology + motivation = Metaphor (skyprickers, skyscrapers, skycities).

This equation, or something like it, should be our starting point. When we name or classify a tall building any number of points may become salient: the vertical surface, the point at the top, the mass, the neo-Gothic style, the technology, the number of people (as represented by the windows) – whatever is brought into the foreground by the designer. Furthermore there is the complexity of the viewpoint. Very few tall buildings can be seen as whole freestanding objects and most are experienced in tight street caverns with one's head stretched back to breaking point. At this angle tall buildings become distorted perspectives, 'railroad tracks' disappearing into whiteness, with a bloated base and a diminutive or unperceivable crown (24). The 'proper' distance to view a 60 storey building is from a quarter of a mile, and thus the paradox arises that the best views of a city are seen when one isn't there. In general the naming of an expressive feature, or the choice of a metaphor, is relative to the characteristic view of a building and any one of the six variables (or their combination) listed in the equation above.

Technical determinants

It *is* a complex affair, and to bring out this complexity we will look at just one part of the equation, the developments in technology, for that area is complex and fascinating enough to stand for the complexity of the five other determinants. Much of this extraordinary and necessary technology we take for granted. Without a revolving door, for instance, a business venture would be ruined everytime the front door of a skyscraper was opened because strong air-currents, created by rising hot air, wind pressure, etc., would wipe the desk-tops clean. For similar reasons flush toilets and vacuum incinerators have saved the skyscraper the indignity of wasteproducts rising dramatically into the air, rather than falling with gravity. The makers of the film *Towering Inferno*, a melodrama featuring various disasters which arise when a tall building burns, overlooked one lugubrious opportunity when they had people fall out not rise up through the burning, central, circulation shaft (as they might if holding umbrellas).

Since tall buildings can sway up to a foot in the wind, all sorts of inventions in wind-bracing and window joinery become necessary to keep people from fainting, or glass walls from popping out (47). If one throws a newspaper from the fortieth storey it will go up. Without the invention of the telephone the skyscraper would be useless as a business venture since messenger boys would be clogging up the elevators. Without advanced lighting, ventilating and cleaning technologies these vertical cities would become unusable. It is worth summarising a few of these necessary innovations and their date of inception.

In 1850 Henry Waterman invented the platform freight elevator and in 1854 Elisha Graves Otis completed his first hydraulic elevator with safety device so that passengers would feel secure. By 1871 passenger elevators were used in office buildings, by 1887 the first electric elevator was in use and by 1904 the first gearless traction elevator was installed. It wasn't until 1924 that the variable voltage elevator allowed quick ·movement (1,100 feet per minute) without noticeable jerks between gears. By then the vertical street had combined with the sealed capsule to produce that characteristic form of city intercourse, the schizophrenic alternation in psychic states, where one is moved from one intense activity to another through moments of relative isolation and silence. Elevator travel had become a welcome respite where one could relax, make up a new face, and prepare a new mood suitable to the next activity. It has become a necessary decompression chamber shunting between discontinuous activities which might otherwise induce hyperactivity: Trader Vics, athletic club, religious instruction, investment banking.

The second major innovations were in structure. Cast-iron was mixed with masonry construction to thin out the ground floor structure of tall buildings and open them up to light and air. This had occurred by the 1870s and it was quickly followed by 'cage construction' and later by 'skeleton construction' (the latter supports the interior *and* exterior walls). By 1885 the steel skeleton had been introduced producing both an immediate saving of 15% on normal building costs and the characteristic grid look — the neutral cage where horizontal and vertical lines were given equal expression. Many theorists became so convinced by the steel skeleton that they made it *the* definer of the skyscraper. The First, Second and now Third 'Chicago Schools' of architecture highlit this feature. Europeans such as Le Corbusier and Siegfried Giedion celebrated it and the South American historian Francisco Mujica made it the basis for his definition of 'firsts'.

> To Jenney (W.L.B.) and Post (George B.) falls the honor of having invented and executed the first metal frames (First Equitable Building in 1871); Jenney has the honor of having built the first embryo skyscraper (Home Life Insurance Company, 1884-5); Hollabird and Roche have somewhat improved this embryo skyscraper (the Tacoma Building); Baumann (Frederick) has the honor of having had the first complete vision of the skeleton skyscraper. Buffington has designed the first building with all-steel frame and the first skyscraper of great height (twenty-eight storey tower in 1888). Burnham and Root (Rand McNally Building in Chicago, 1889) have the honor of having constructed the first all-steel frame skyscraper and the honor which falls to all of them together as inventors and initiators of the steel skeleton skyscraper belongs to the United States of America.[4]

It's an inspiring roll-call conveying that sense of pride and naivety which accompanied these pioneering endeavours. It was followed by a cooler look at the expression of structure, not just its first use, and this led to the tradition of tall buildings which could be called 'skycages' (41, 44). James Bogardus used the iron skeleton in New York in 1848, but then the skycage moved to Chicago where it turned into the 'Chicago frame', the 'Commercial Style', the 'prison cage', 'grid paper', 'skin and bones' and finally 'exoskeleton'. In and out of favour it went. First praised for its pragmatism, then damned for its philistinism; next celebrated for its honesty, then villified for its boredom. The skycage became a matter of design principle with William Le Baron Jenney, Louis Sullivan and later the Europeans such as Hilberseimer and Max Taut who romanticised its neutral purity, especially in their entries to the Chicago Tribune Competition, 1922.

Actually, the projection of the neutral, two-way grid onto the surface is only one of many options open to the designer of skeleton constructions, and the others depend on the size of the building and the visual goals of the designer. With improvements in rolled steel sections (1900), riveting, welding, and the invention of floating foundations, pressurised concrete piles and caisson foundations (1893), with the theoretical developments in structures (1930-1960), a host of optimum solutions was created. The structural diagram (ii), produced in Chicago in the mid-sixties shows some of the 'best' options for steel at various storeys. The critical factor in most cases is wind-bracing. Since the tall building can be regarded as a thin tube cantilevered into space, which will bend because of 100 mile per hour winds and pressure differentials, it has to be calculated as a long structure fixed at the ground undergoing lateral stresses. Above 70 storeys one form of tube or another is the most economic as it places most of the structure on the outside to create the greatest moment of inertia. Between this outer load-bearing wall and the interior core is then a column-free span. It's ironic that through technological progress we have arrived, with the tallest buildings in the world (75,82) back in the 1880s with load-bearing walls, but then the history of the skyscraper often shows such recurrences.

The Sears Tower in Chicago (82) with its 114 storeys is a set of nine bundled tubes, with various banks of express elevators running within each segment. The John Hancock Center (24), another example of Chicago's technological fatalism, is a combination of a widely spaced tube wall and diagonal truss bracing. This combination cut the cost of supply and erection of steel to half of that used in the comparable Chase Manhattan Bank in New York – and it remains a most economic type. It also produces an amusing set of visual contradictions and juxtapositions. Heavy diagonals cut through the living-room wall, corner windows diminish oddly with increasing height and the vertical expression of piers is counterpointed by criss-cross bays. This contradiction, which gives scale and interest, can be suppressed by internal, diagonal bracing which occurs between the shear core and external columns. And this solution, which Philip Johnson has used on the IDS Building (iii and cover), can be more efficient as it only has to be used every 20 or 30 storeys.

Structural expressionism, and its inherent metaphors of skycage, skytube and skytruss, tends to become more inevitable after 70 storeys when the structural expense becomes significant. As if doubtful of the building standing above this height, architects and their clients have wanted to express structure above all other concerns. They are swayed by the engineer's aesthetic and the cost-benefit analyst and the two together nearly produce the whole image. A little

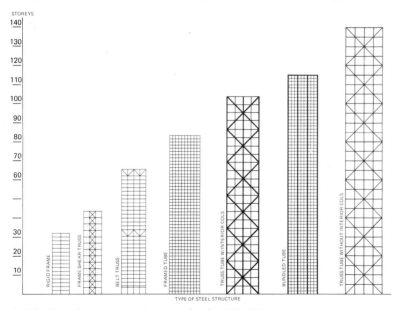

ii Suitability of steel structural systems for the tall building.

room for fantasy, however, is left for the corporation and the designer. Minoru Yamasaki gives his two, 110 storey 'tubes' a glistening expression in stainless steel and pseudo-Gothic arches – a memory of Woolworth Gothic (66) and the age when shooting at the sky was an act of mercantile faith.

Less visually provocative but no less important than the developments of the elevator and steel structures, were the innovations in fire protection, lighting and ventilating. Perhaps because of the Chicago fire in 1871, innovations in fire resistant devices occurred there before New York: the hollow tile floor (1872), the covering of all columns and beams with heat resistant tiles and then finally, by the turn of the century, the use of spray-on asbestos. Recent developments of intumescent paint coatings and concrete/water-filled sections further protect the steel from bending under extreme heat.[5] They also allow the designer to express the exoskeleton.

Natural lighting determinants – twenty-seven feet from the window to the core presumed to be the maximum allowable distance, in the case of the RCA Building – have often fixed the stepped profiles of large buildings, so that they naturally step back when each elevator bank is dropped (72).

It wasn't until 1948 and the Equitable Savings and Loan Building that the first environmentally-sealed building was created. This combined the heating, ventilating and lighting systems in one closed, self-sufficient package. From then on the hermetically-sealed skyscraper, with fifty-foot window-core distances, became common and it is only recently, responding to public desires, that designers have once again provided the occasional window that opens.

Because of the very deep plans which the new technologies allowed, a deep ceiling which housed these mechanisms became a reality and one which could be expressed, along with the structure, on the exterior. Hence the horizontal rhythm of 'large/small' which the Lever Building established and which became the norm in the fifties (41). Philip Johnson has taken this alternating pattern to an extreme and exaggerated the difference between servant and served space in the horizontal 'skycake' in Houston (42). Another option is expressing the air-conditioning plants on various floors. The United Nations Building, 1947-53, with its various horizontal bands and grills is an early example of the 'skyslab' which is divided neatly into well-proportioned chunks by floors of mechanical equipment. The placement of these floors is a matter of some choice by the designer. Often they are at the top and bottom of the building thus reinforcing the metaphor of 'skycolumn', a major metaphor for the tall building as we will see. Or, as in the case of Johnson's IDS Center already mentioned, the mechanical equipment can be placed on two floors and combined with the internal cross-bracing, because fans and ducts, as opposed to people, don't mind diagonals shooting through the floor (iii).

To generalise then about technological determinism, its effect on the tall building and its metaphors, we arrive at a tautology: the techniques determine the image of the building in so far as the designer and client wish it and they tend to wish it over 70 storeys or in

very wide 'squat scrapers', when the volume of a building is larger than average. In short this is determinism plus free-will, social coercion and fashion – what could be called weak determinism to distinguish it from the absolute variety. It is an important part of our equation, as a quick description of the Chrysler Building will show, but only one significant part.

Mixed metaphors

The Chrysler Building, 1928-30, was one of those great New York buildings that was World Famous, and Tallest for a Short Time (the Empire State topped it in 1931, and there are six Ex-World's Tallest illustrated in this book). According to a monograph produced at the time it had the following numerical characteristics among many others: it was (and is) 77 storeys tall, it occupies an entire block of 37,555 square feet with 1,000,000 square feet of floor area and a daily population of 10,000 tenants and employees.[6] It requires 350 attendants to care for the tenancy and 150 to vacuum clean it every night, with 50 feet of wandering hose for every cleaning point. Because of the large amounts of waste created by 10,000 typists and the difficulty of hauling this mountain of verbiage away from midtown Manhattan a special destructor plant was built that can chew up '800 pounds per hour of miscellaneous rubbish, including up to 20% by weight of wet restaurant garbage'. It can also handle temporary peak loads of 1,120 pounds per hour when tenants move in (and presumably clean up after the office party).

Two independent air-conditioning systems were provided, a heavy duty drainage system which could handle 100 gallons of water a minute, thick sound-proofing between elevators and usable space, 32 elevators which can rise 1,000 feet per minute, '21,000 tons of structural steel, 391,881 rivets, 3,826,000 bricks, 446,000 pieces of tile, 794,000 pieces of partition block, 3,750 plate glass windows, 200 sets of stairs, 2/5ths of a mile of aluminium railings, 35 miles of pipe, 15 miles of brass strip for joining terrazzo floors, 750 miles of electric conductor wire' (one tenant alone has 1,000 telephone connections). It is obvious from this partial list that any skyscraper must also be a metaphor of *repetition*, whatever else it is. In the case of the Chrysler these other aspects concern the three salient points of the vertical building: its base, shaft and capital (crown or crest).

The base, as in many skyscrapers, is actually a complex form in itself, which is responding to contradictory pressures. It fills out the site almost completely to the sixteenth floor, responding to the pressure of maximum rentable area near the ground (iv). Then with

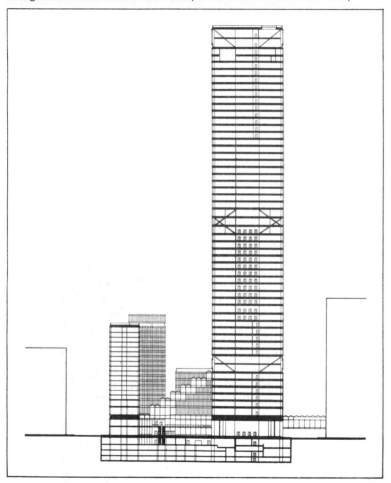

iii PHILIP JOHNSON and JOHN BURGEE, *I.D.S. Center*, Minneapolis, Minnesota, 1972-5, section.

two more setbacks and a transitional horizontal base it finally reaches the 'shaft' on the thirtieth storey. Thus we have *four* heavy bases to our 'column' and these bases resemble a stepped 'ziggurat' on one side, and a U-shaped 'palazzo' on the other. It is worth stressing these mixed metaphors not only because they are the rule in skyscrapers, but also because critics tend to overlook their complexity while they classify the more simple tripartite metaphor, the 'column'.[7]

The 'capital' of this, which has attracted so much attention and which epitomises 'skyscraping' for many is also a mixed metaphor. One writer, Claude Bradgon, referred to it in 1932 as a frozen fountain: 'A building a fountain: how clarifying a point of view! . . . The needle-pointed *flèche* of the Chrysler tower catches the sunlight like a fountain's highest expiring jet'.[8] Fountain and *flèche*, to these images are added others by the Chrysler monograph: it is a 'lofty crown', a 'beacon that flashes a message of high achievement by day and night', a 'finial spire' and a 'coronet of Nirosta steel . . . which will reflect the passing clouds and blend the tower into the sky'.[9] Crown, beacon, spire, skyblender, needle, fountain and, perhaps, 'halo' and 'sunburst'? The top 7 storeys, tapered in echelons and semi-circles of Nirosta steel, also resemble a futurist hat and one in fact worn by the architect, William van Alen, at a Beaux-Arts Costume Ball in 1931.[10] Actually the architect, when he first designed the top in 1928, conceived of it as a more traditional form: 'A glass dome, which, when lighted from within, will give the effect of a great jewelled sphere'.[11] And we can still see this submerged metaphor of the 'glowing dome' at night, when the swell of the curved echelons is more apparent, in spite of the fact that the design went through two more transformations.

A new typology

The Chrysler Building is in sum an extreme example of what most skyscrapers are: a mixed metaphor and a complex building morphology which incorporates palace, slab, setback, column, tower and spire. To make sense of this heterogeneity and give some logic to the metaphors, we must adopt a basic typology. Winston Wiseman, in the article previously mentioned, attempts a typology and ties it to evolutionary stages.[12] He finds seven phases which can be generalised roughly as follows: 1) the *preskyscraper* phase (1849-70) when the essential elements are present but not assembled into one building; 2) the *early* phase when the basic four elements are present (elevator, structure, sufficient height, business function) but older compositional features are used (1868-70); 3) the *flat-roofed* phase with free

iv WILLIAM VAN ALEN, *Chrysler Building*, New York, 1928-20.

and composed groupings of storeys (1878-1920?); 4) the *tripartite* phase of the 'column' building (1880-present?); 5) the *tower* phase (1888-95) made up of 'isolated' (1888) and 'mounted' (1911, but actually before) and 'setback' (from the zoning codes of 1916 to the present); 6) the *setback* phase dictated by zoning codes (1916 to the present); 7) the *multiblock* phase dating from the Rockefeller Center (1930-present).

As a broad categorisation of New York and Chicago trends this typology is illuminating but it has several problems in addition to the ones of definition and expression already mentioned. The tripartite phase, when looked at closer, often is a quadripartite structure or has more divisions than three, as does the Chrysler Building. Furthermore this 'column', when multiplied sideways, changes into a 'slab' or 'palace', as in Louis Sullivan's Wainwright Building (35). For the same kind of reasons the 'mounted tower' both appears before the date mentioned (1911) and also merges imperceptibly with the 'setback' solution – which therefore has to be given earlier dates (Adler and Sullivan's Auditorium Building, 1887-9). Lastly there are no terminal dates to these phases, as Wiseman avers, and as Philip Johnson's recently designed AT & T warns us (it uses the columnar organisation). The biggest problem, however, is the hybrid nature of most skyscrapers and this complexity which leads to the mixed metaphors.

Thus we might proceed from a new typological scheme and add to it more complex articulations of style, technology etc. as they become relevant, always remembering that the ultimate metaphor is based on an interaction of the six variables listed in the equation above, the angle of view we choose and the visual codes of the viewer. Basic to classifying is the overall morphology of the building as seen from a bird's-eye perspective (a rare view except from the Empire State Building). There are three fundamental plan types perceivable from this position: the *centralised* form with its circulation core at the centre, the *longitudinal* form with its circulation off-centre and sometimes near the ends, and the *compound* form with several circulation points located variably. These are the three basic types (generating skyprickers, skyscrapers and skycities) which subsume all other metaphors.[13]

The centralised form developed from obelisks, spires and pyramids although of course they had no internal circulation to speak of, and it became a usable building type with the defensive tower and campanile. From the centralised form has developed the *skypricker* and its many variants: skypagodas and skyneedles etc. If a centralised form is projected up it naturally becomes a skycolumn; if it tapers inwards to a point it becomes a skypricker. For these reasons it is one of our three logical types. Yet if the surface is articulated with cage construction, or if the exterior is undulated, or if the style is neo-Gothic, we may overlook the centralising form and classify by a more visible feature. Hence the metaphors skypalace and skycathedral may be paradoxically seen in this form, metaphors which are logically more suited to the linear or compound form. The ultimate paradox of this class, the skylump, the centralised building that never grows much higher than it is wide, is actually a common form of 'tall' building (63, left). It is kept lumpy for obvious reasons of cost and efficiency; the maximum occupation of a lot near the ground.

The skypricker is a logical type because of its internal organisation and circulation, but it tends to become a slab when put on a city block because of the width of the lot, the internal light and ventilation requirements and, often, the available real estate (rectangular lots generate slabs). Linear slabs are the most common form of tall building and have been since the 1870s. When they touch the sky with their long edge they 'scrape' like a knife. Thus we may deduce the inherent urban law that every skypricker wants to become a skyscraper; or that every skycolumn wants to be extruded sideways for maximum rentable value in order to become a skypalace. Indeed tall buildings of the 1900s, such as the Flatiron Building in New York City, can be seen as columns from the corner and as palaces from the side (34).

The *skyscraper*, or the ideal-type longitudinal building, can again take on many other metaphors depending on the surface articulation, style and use. As a slab it can step up and down as in the RCA Building (72), or fracture out or curve as in the Toronto City Hall. Most strikingly, it can pinch at the corners and become the skywedge, which, in the Pirelli Building both scrapes and slices clouds (46). The two skywedges of Philip Johnson in Houston (77) also have a very dramatic cutting profile as two black meat cleavers seen against the sky, and the prevalence of triangular or sharp-edged tall buildings should warn us that every skyscraper wants to become a skyknife; if only it were economical. The more pragmatic shape and hence the major type of longitudinal building has been, since the 1870s, the complex slab. Louis Sullivan and others in Chicago worked out the major variants based on double-loaded corridors and light wells. These have been plans with I, L, T, U, H, E and ∓shapes. Frank Lloyd Wright and Verner Moser developed the last mentioned shape, with its finger extensions off the main slab, in schemes for the National Life Insurance Company of Chicago, 1924.[14] The problem with these pragmatic shapes is that they cut down exterior views and light.

So far the ultimate skyscraper is I.M. Pei and Henry Cobb's John Hancock Building in Boston (47-52). Because of its slab shape it slices the clouds, because of its angled facets it serrates them into thin slices, and because of its precise mirror-finish edge it slices them more finely than other knives. Another highly expressive aspect to this building is its blue-mirror finish. Since it is set in an area of Boston, Copley Square, which has a rich variety of buildings, open space and trees, it becomes much more variable in image than other reflective buildings. Sometimes it reflects H.H. Richardson's heavy masonry church, from other views it acts as a foil to the dark-red roofs; sometimes it can reflect entirely the old John Hancock Building next door; while other times its blue glass can merge with the sky. The 'skybergs', to name these quixotic mirrored buildings, are light-sensitive and can give as many shades and tones and moods as can the changing sky. Watching the sunset in the reflection of a skyberg is as interesting as watching it set in reality (and less damaging to the eye).

If the skypricker wants to become a skyscraper because of economic and formal pressure, then the skyscraper wants to become a *skycity* for the same reasons. Philip Johnson's IDS Center in Minneapolis illustrates this tendency and, again, its attendant problem for any typology and metaphorical classification. From the plan (v) it is clear that the centralised skypricker has become a longitudinal skyscraper and then swallowed further compound types on the lot. The most notable type is the covered 'atrium' space, what Johnson calls variously 'cave', 'crystal court' and 'living-room of the city'.[15] Where should we place this mixed metaphor? The tower alone has base, shaft and capital and the sides of the shaft are fluted – so it's a skycolumn. But this column merges with the stepped atrium which fits, in turn, into two more serrated slabs. Looked at from above the column dominates; from below the facets and slabs are most visible, another illustration of the way viewpoint determines classification and metaphor (cover).

In any case the compound tall building, the skycity, is the third major type and one which has enjoyed a popularity since the building of the Rockefeller Center Complex in the thirties. Winston Wiseman traces the multiblock solution to this scheme, but again we can find earlier historical precedents: San Gimignano with its 72 towers was a skycity in the fourteenth century (59). So, in a sense, were the 'mounted towers' of New York City, the Tribune Building, 1873-5, the Metropolitan Tower, 1909, and the Woolworth Building, 1911-3 (66). Mounted towers, tower and slab, twin towers and clustered towers should, I believe, be considered as a distinctive morphological type which shares a compound shape and variable circulation pattern. It generates the skycity and its offspring, many of which are relatives of the two previous types: e.g. skycathedral*s*, skypalace*s* and sky-wedge*s* (the plural of groups one and two). This stretching of metaphor across morphological types again shows that no one point of our equation can act as an absolute variable for classification. To clarify this equation and the overlap of metaphor I have provided the following diagram. It shows that the three major morphological types do generate clusters of different metaphors, but in no rigorous sense (vi).

Substitution of metaphors

In order to summarise the significance of this diagram, another typological approach has to be considered. In an interesting article on the

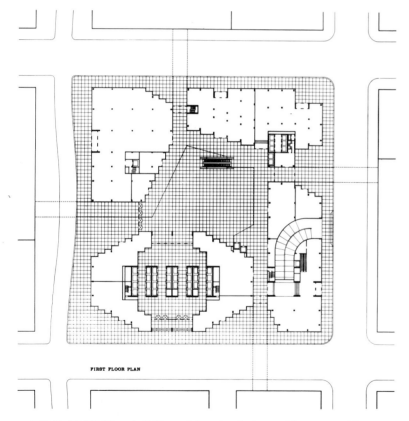

FIRST FLOOR PLAN

v PHILIP JOHNSON and JOHN BURGEE, *I.D.S. Center*, Minneapolis, Minnesota, 1972-5, first floor plan.

vi METAPHORICAL EQUATION

SKYPRICKER		SKYSCRAPER		SKYCITIES	
skypagoda	skyneedle	*skyknife*	*skycage*	skypalaces	*skycrowns*
skypin	skyskewer	*skywedge*	*skyberg*	skyaedicules	skycolum*ns*
skycolumn	skytemple	skymirror	skygrave	skytemples	skybottles
skyziggurat	skyobelisk	*skypalace*	skyblob	skyblobs	*skyspires*
skytower	skytube	skyutensils	skyjump	skysquatters	skytubes
skytable	skypeople	*skycathedral*	skycake	skytriangles	
skycrown	skylump	*skytruss*	*skytube*	skybundles	*skylumps*
skytool	skyholder	skycutter		skycakes	skycathedra*ls*
skyshoot	*skycake*	skyscratcher		skygraves	*skyclusters*
skyrailroad	skyjump	skyrepetition		skyholders	skypeople

‖ ‖ ‖

1) MORPHOLOGY

CENTRAL	LONGITUDINAL	COMPOUND
square tower	slab	compound tower/slab
round tower	stepped slab	complex tower/slab
ziggurat tower	curved slab	double tower/slab
triangular etc.	shaped slab	compound towers/slabs
shaped tower	amorphous slab	cluster tower/slabs
compound tower	complex slab	
	(E,T,U,X,etc.)	

+

2) ARTICULATION OF SURFACE

a) horizontal/vertical, b) heavy/light, c) complex/simple, d) geometric/amorphous, e) expressive/dumb,

f) reflective/absorptive, g) structural/skin-like membrane, h) top-pointed, flat, complex.

+

3) STYLE

a) Mansardic 1870, b) classical 1880, c) Queen Anne 1880, d) Chicago frame, Commercial Style 1890,

e) Tower-like 1890, f) Neo-Gothic 1900, g) Art Deco 1925, h) International Style 1930, i) Brutalist 1965,

j) Late-Modern 1965, k) Post-Modern 1970.

+

4) ACTIVITY

a) defensive, b) religious, c) business, d) commercial, e) residential, f) multiple.

+

5) TECHNOLOGY

a) elevator, b) structural capability, c) fire protection, d) lighting e) electricity, f) cleaning, g) heating and

ventilating and cooling.

+

6) MOTIVATION

a) monument, b) land value, c) power.

meaning of skyscrapers Diana Agrest has argued that skyscraper history shows a 'circulation of meanings' between base, shaft and crest, that is between elements of the skycolumn.

The transformation by which the crest cedes its symbolic role first to the entire building and then to the base can be exemplified by three instances: the 'spires' of the St. Mark's and Price Towers by Frank Lloyd Wright [20]; Hugh Ferriss' setback skyscraper where the whole building becomes a crest; and finally the case where the body or shaft becomes the whole building thereby eliminating the symbolic crest entirely. The last case is really a mutation of the first, in which the building as crest is transformed into a base thereby foreclosing one transformation and opening the next... [Later, by 1962] The meaningful relationship now becomes the space between the buildings, and their repetition now becomes the essential aspect of the meaning. This is clear in the World Trade Center [75], where the 'tallest building' is actually two buildings, and the crest as symbol has been metonymically replaced by a double aspect: repetition and the space between considered as form in itself.[16]

The last point may be questioned. In what *important* sense is a 'crest' replaced by twin towers and the space between them? Just because one element of a complex equation is lost and another is gained does not mean that a significant substitution has occurred. There are many other changes as well, in the buildings she cites, and enough of them to rule out any one-to-one substitution. And yet the notion of substitution itself seems fruitful if we generalise it across all typologies and metaphors (not just the tripartite skycolumn). For an incessant substitution of one metaphor for another is continuously found in tall building history. Skyprickers become skyscrapers become skycities become skyprickers, and all of these types mingle, cohabit and produce their many variants. In every case one expressive sign is substituted for another, while competition, architectural skill and capitalism drive the substitution on further and further. In all of this incessant change and circulation of types, in all this utilitarian activity motivated by profit, it is comforting to think that metaphor and expression play a primary role — for they are what make the building distinctive and hence a saleable item.

This relationship between function, profit motive and expression recalls one of the few statements by a designer on the expressive role of the skyscraper. Louis Sullivan published an article in 1896 called 'The Tall Office Building Artistically Considered', in which he formulated the tripartite skycolumn based on both functional and expressive qualities.

The practical conditions are, broadly speaking, these: Wanted: first, a storey below ground, containing boilers, engines of various sorts, etc., — in short, the plant for power, heating, lighting, etc.; second, a ground floor, so called, devoted to

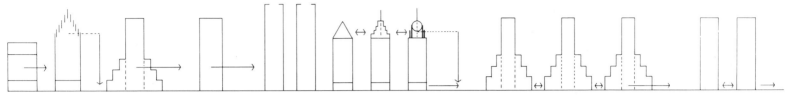

vii Comparison of morphological types of tall buildings.

stores, banks, or other establishments requiring large areas, ample spacing, ample light, and great freedom of access; third, a second storey readily accessible by stairways, this space usually in large sub-divisions, with corresponding liberality in structural spacing and expanse of glass and breadth of external openings; fourth, above this an indefinite number of storeys of offices piled tier upon tier, one tier just like another tier, one office just like all the other offices, an office being similar to a cell in a honeycomb, merely a compartment, nothing more; fifth and last, at the top of this pile is placed a space or storey that, as related to the life and usefulness of the structure, is purely physiological in its nature, namely the attic . . .

What is the chief characteristic of the tall office building? And at once we answer, it is lofty. This loftiness is to the artist-nature its thrilling aspect. It is the very open organ-tone of its appeal. It must be in turn the dominant chord in his expression of it, the true excitant of his imagination. It must be tall. The force and power of altitude must be in it, the glory and pride of exaltation must be in it. It must be every inch a proud and soaring thing, rising in sheer exultation that from bottom to top it is a unit without a single dissenting line . . . [17]

Here is what many people feel to be the essence of the skyscraper; its 'loftiness'; a 'proud and soaring thing'. Indeed these are the special expressive qualities of the skycolumns that Sullivan designed, as they bring out their inherent vertical morphology and reach to the sky. One can only take partial exception to this description because it excludes the variety of expressive types (e.g. skycakes *with* dissenting lines), but it is nevertheless an exceptional statement because it insists on the visual expression and symbolism of the tall building. This is what I have tried to do in a more general way: concentrate on the main expressive types and give them names.

Yet behind all this manifest imagery is a hidden symbol, the grand metaphor which is always implicit in every tall building, the unspoken assumption between architect and client which doesn't care to be named. A story, perhaps apocryphal, about the commissioning of the Transamerica Building conveys this latent meaning. The architect William Pereira was presenting six different schemes for this building to a group of executives from the company. They pored over the plans and elevations placed on a large conference table; they debated the cost and imagery of different solutions, but there was no single scheme which convinced the group as a whole because they were all variations on a conventional skyblob. Pereira had in fact designed a seventh scheme, an old skyscraper project of which he was particularly fond and one which had been rejected several times previously by other corporations because of its extreme pointedness. When the committee was deadlocked they turned to Pereira for advice. Which scheme should he develop, which should he combine? Pereira shrugged indifferently waiting for the anxiety to increase. Then he allowed: 'I have a seventh scheme, but you wouldn't want to see it.' 'Yes', they answered like a chorus from the *Frogs*. He pulled from underneath the table his seventh scheme, the one he always wanted, and slowly unrolled a tapering, rising, piercing skypricker, the present Transamerica Building with its upward thrusting wedges (22). Here it was pointing skywards optimistically like rising corporate spirits and rising corporate profits to be located in the clouds, a symbol of triumph. And this is what it has always meant. The symbol of corporate power, the rising up of real estate, services, production, the variety of city functions integrated for a single end – a 'capital symbol'. This is what drives all the changing metaphors of scraping and pricking and cutting and slicing and shooting. These last are the acceptable faces of what might finally be renamed 'skyplunders'. They seek in their ever-increasing height to overcome all previous building types, all the pyramids and cathedrals of the past, as indeed all recent records of height. Profit and power are tied by architects to a Nietzschean symbolism that both prophecies and seeks to bring about a future world order that is more strong and brilliant than any in the past. The new social order may be forever on the horizon and the next World's Tallest may be always about to arrive on stage, but these pressures of self-transcendence are not discouraging; they merely confirm the Utopian streak deep in the heart of society.

Skyprickers and skyneedles. The centralised skypricker has many historical precedents which designers of the nineteenth and twentieth century modified to their purpose. Pagados, obelisks and steeples were the most obvious precedents for the heavenly-soaring building. Pagados, with their odd number of diminishing tiers, have a rocket-like thrust toward the sky — accentuated by upturned eaves, or in the case of the Bangkok Temple, by sweeping curves. Coloured, glistening ceramic and stylised brackets (made in stone to imitate wood) seem to add a shimmering power of ascent to the pagodas. The 218 foot Temple of Dawn spire (a Cambodian type known as a 'prang') has multicoloured porcelain embedded in its surface which shimmers in strong sunlight. Ordinarily the upper storeys could not be reached and their function was to mark, monumentally, a relic or shrine. Steeples and spires had a similar monumental function. In the case of Chartres their sharp ascent, under-scored by further pinnacles, really does seem to prick the sky. The bottom of the south tower, begun in 1145 in the Early Gothic Style, is surmounted by pairs of windows and colon-nettes and then, above the square plan, by projecting tabernacles and the sharp octagonal spire. The transformation of vertical forms again seems to increase the upward move-ment.

1 *Temple Pagoda, Xu Mi Fu Shou*, Chengde, built for the Emperor Chien Lung's 70th birthday (7 storeys), 1780.
2 *Temple of Dawn, Wat Arun*, Bangkok, 1765-1800. (Geoffrey Broadbent)
3 *Chartres Cathedral*, north tower 1134, north spire 1507, south tower begun 1145, rose window early XIII century.

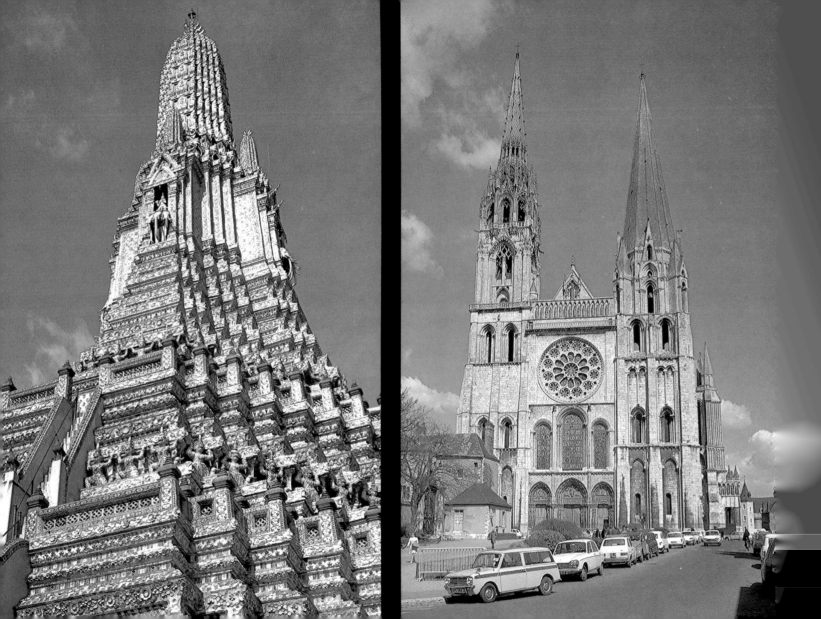

The centralised, New York tall building often ended in a sharp point or series of points as here, becoming a skypalace or skycathedral. In both cases the need for a romantic crown or crest was felt; an emphatic ending to the vertical movement. This might carry out a theme started on the bottom floor. Henry J. Hardenbergh, the designer of the Dakota and the Plaza Hotel, has finished off the latter building with an eclectic mixture of images. Twin aedicules, little palaces in the sky, built of white, glazed brick, are to either side of a Renaissance arcade and green-copper-and-slate mansard roof. The green copper relates to other buildings in the area (as well as visually to the fountain), while the overall urban mass of the hotel forms an important, monumental pivot to the plaza on one side and Central Park at right angles. It holds the street line and turns the corner, with its round towers, with a heavy, Edwardian, convincing ponderousness. Diagonally opposite the Sherry-Netherland Hotel ends with an even more romantic aedicule, a little hideaway that has steep roofs, Romanesque gables, a lantern and gargoyles all set into a wild, asymmetrical spin. It caps the slender brick tower with an emphatic prick.

4 HENRY J. HARDENBERGH, *The Plaza Hotel*, New York City, 1907.
5, 6 SCHULTZE and WEAVER, *Sherry-Netherland Hotel*, New York City, 1927. (Close-up Giampietro Parboni).

Skycathedrals, or more simply the Gothic Revival Style, led to the later morphology of tall buildings as the examples on these and the next four pages show. It combined with the Art Deco Style, the zigzags, setbacks and extreme vertical emphasis, to be epitomised in the thirties by the Empire State Building and in the sixties by the World Trade Center. Here we can see early and middle stages of that evolution. Big Ben, the 316 foot tower (equivalent to a 30 storey building), carries on the mixture of horizontal and vertical exphasis of the Houses of Parliament, itself a mixture of Tudor-Gothic detail over a classical grid. The swell near the top, surrounding the clock, surmounted by a double crown, gives this tower a pleasing top-heavy emphasis, a very dramatic ending to vertical movement which finds an echo in later tall buildings (63). The Chicago Tribune Tower, 1922-5, epitomises the vertically articulated skycathedral with its very thin shafts, its alternating bay rhythm and its triple crown of flying buttresses and 'Late Gothic' fretwork (which repeats that of the base). The building thus illustrates the favourite skycolumn theme of base, shaft and capital.

7 SIR CHARLES BARRY and AUGUSTUS W.N. PUGIN, *Big Ben*, London, 1858-9.
8, 9 RAYMOND HOOD & JOHN M. HOWELLS, *Chicago Tribune Tower*,

Skyfurnace was the implicit metaphor behind this 21 storey tower designed by Raymond Hood as a combination of his Chicago Tribune Tower, Eliel Saarinen's second-place winner for the competition and the Woolworth Building (66). The building was for the American Radiator Company which made furnaces and heaters and so it was conceived as a gigantic advertisement for their products: at night the gold terracotta crown is lit by floodlights so it glows like a torch. During the day the radiator effect is still pronounced due to the massive, black detailing and sparkling top. Indeed Hood used black brick 'to prevent undue contrast for the countless windows in what might destroy the mass silhouette'. This heavyweight tradition of tall buildings was given a new twist by Mies' Seagrams (44). Here Raymond Hood cantilevered and bevelled the corners, as well as stepped them back, to increase the apparent size of this relatively small building. The tower with windows thus remained visually a totality unlike other tall offices. This gives it a strong vertical presence especially since it can be seen from afar, across Bryant Park (with its later offspring the Empire State Building looking over its shoulder).

10, 11 HOOD & FOUILHOUX, *American-Standard Building* (originally

Skytools became operative instruments to advertise both the product and the idea of the tall building as a blown-up piece of domestic equipment. The old 51 storey RCA Victor Building is a scratchy type of victrola needle at the top, while on the bottom and sides vibrating needles (held up by hands) seem the ultimate in electrical energy (happily for its imagery the building was taken over by General Electric). The crown is an intermixture of gilded radio waves, Gothic fretwork and Art Deco zaps. The base has equally zany forced marriages between scrawny hands and electric lights, G-clefts and vine tendrils, expressionist brick-work and *ad hoc* left-overs. In comparison the Eastern Building in Los Angeles is sober — except for its colour contrasts: light green greasy terracotta, darker blue flutings and golden highlights. The giant clock gives the game away like the RCA Victor needles: it's really an oversize parking meter.

12, 13 CROSS & CROSS, *GE Building* (originally *RCA Victor*), New York, 1931.
14 CLAUDE BEELMAN, *The Eastern (now 849) Building*, Los Angeles, 1929.

Skycolumns, or table legs holding the sky, reappear regularly in the history of tall buildings and three hybrid examples are illustrated here (which underscores the point that metaphorical classification is rarely pure and hardly simple). The two New York buildings to the left are slender towers in half their length and complex, double bases for the other part. This distortion of the column is made for quite obvious, contradictory reasons of maximum floor area (near the ground) and maximum height and expression (the top). The Texas tower (right) also sits on a base, but its vertical, columnar expression more clearly predominates with window 'fluting' accenting the center lines to be taken up in the clock and broken pediment. The top crown, a little temple in itself, can be seen as a miniature of the whole building thus making the 'capital' also a tripartite column. The Fuller Building for the head office of a construction firm mixes black, white and grey masonry with Art Deco octogons, Aztec motifs and Herculean construction workers in a Mannerist set of contradictory visual directions (horizontal sides, vertical centres). 500 Fifth Avenue is a simpler building and a dry run for the later Empire State Building by the same architects, but it also mixes advertising motifs and complex geometries.

15 WALKER & GILLETTE, *Fuller Building*, New York, 1928-9.
16 SHREVE, LAMB & HARMON, *500 Fifth Avenue*, New York, 1931.
17 PAUL CRET, *Main Building*, University of Texas, Austin, 1933.

Ultimate Skyprickers, the result of a 3,000 year transformation of the obelisk and spire until they finally became the usable building. The Chrysler (see text for a technical description, page 10) was the world's tallest building for a few months, the Empire State for more than thirty years. Then 'The Biggest' left New York, its usual place of occupation, and moved to Chicago (82). Both buildings are skycolumns whose capital recapitulates the overall form; both use stainless steel ('never grows dull') on a scale at the top which makes them beacons, and lighthouses at night. The mixed metaphors applied to the Chrysler crown (frozen fountain, flèche, beacon, needle, halo, sunburst, glowing dome, coronet, skyblender) are somewhat different from those of the Empire State (inverted test-tube, landlocked light-house, mooring mast, radio antennae), but there is no doubt what these tops do to the clouds: puncture them. The Chrysler, 1,048 feet to the 77 storey top, has Art Deco stainless steel hub caps, radiator cap wings, eagle gargoyles and triangular facets radiating from a center line. In the 'spire-dome' was Walter Chrysler's duplex apartment, an observatory, gymnasium and 'Cloud Club' for business lunches. The Empire State Building, 1,250 feet, 67 elevators, ultimately holding 25,000 people, was not rented when it was finished during the Depression and was relabelled 'The Empty State Building'. The graceful silhouette in different cool greys was meant to enhance the 'upward sweep' as were the shadowless windows flush with the surface. Once the initial decisions were made the building completed itself in a year and a half, an example, as Rem Koolhaas has argued, of 'automatic architecture'.

18 WILLIAM VAN ALEN, *Chrysler Building*, New York, 1928-30.
19 SHREVE, LAMB & HARMON, *Empire State Building*, New York, 1929-31,

Geometrical counterpoint became a theme of fifties and sixties tall buildings with Frank Lloyd Wright showing the way with
a scheme, the Price Tower, which he had designed in the late
twenties. This building is made from 90° geometries rotated 45°
to each other; where the two geometries break through at the
surface a counterpoint is set up between horizontal and vertical
green fins. These articulate different areas: the vertical mullions
indicate living areas punctuated by balconies, the horizontal
fins and sunshades mark the office space, while stairs, toilets
and kitchen are located behind the more enclosed surface.
When these geometries are stacked vertically, given an alter-
nate banding of concrete and green copper spandrels, and
allowed to erupt into sharp wall fins on the top, one has the
most expressive skypricker and skyscraper of our century. By
comparison the geometrical simplicities of Welton Beckett and
William Pereira are too obvious; yet they still are an alternative
to the 'dumb box'. Capitol Records is, inevitably, a series of
round floor plans, stacked records on a victrola, with a diamond
needle poised to one side. The Transamerica Pyramid, with its
truss at the bottom and counterpoint between solid shaft, solid
top and open middle, is more interesting and it has become the
most recognisable high building in San Francisco.

Skyleg and skytruss shoot railroad tracks to the clouds; structural supports on the outside have an old fashioned role as a load-bearing wall. These buildings are truncated skyprickers because of their centralised geometry, even though they don't end in a point. The CBS Building creates weird, mordant patterns, an alternation of dark granite, black shadow and black glass in parallel vertical rows. Because the piers are triangular and set on an angle to the viewer they have a sharp, speedy ascent, quickened by their close spacing; each one is an ultra-thin version of the whole building. Because the building has no real bottom and top articulation, but rises sheer, it is a skyleg rather than a skycolumn. Absence of articulation takes on a value here since it is so pronounced: it is a column which is 'all fluting'. Expressive substitution of one metaphor for another is the dynamic of tall building development, a fact which can be seen when we compare the John Hancock Building in Chicago to the CBS. Now the black centralised tower has been bent towards the pyramid to associate with this form as well as increase the perspective diminishment (this creates odd window angles every so often). A pleasing counterpoint is set up between the diagonal truss and rectangular bays. Both buildings illustrate the 1960s metaphor 'skin and bones'.

23 EERO SAARINEN & ASSOCIATES, *CBS Building*, New York, 1965.
24, 25 BRUCE GRAHAM & SOM (Chicago), *John Hancock Center*, Chicago, 1969.

The shaped, centralised building usually takes on a regular geometric figure although there are many free-form schemes. Two of these by Mies Van der Rohe in the early twenties were models for the Lake Point Tower, erected by his followers in Chicago. The Y-plan of this building does away with the 'problem of the corner' (the problem of turning an internal junction) by curving it away. This self-contained city with its variety of community activities (including horseback riding) protects itself with high walls, security guards and other paraphernalia of gracious living. Bronze tinted glass which filters out excessive heat and glare is common to the 'skin' solution: the Noa Building, next to Tokyo's 'Eiffel Tower', juxtaposes this against sheer brick and concrete. The Crédit Lyonnais crowns the skytube with a pyramid and brightly lit internal space, an early example of the Post-Modern tall building. The exterior grid of sun-blinds is articulated at various points to give scale and divisibility to the facade.

26 SCHIPPOREIT/HEINRICH ASSOCIATES, *Lake Point Tower*, Chicago, 1968-9. (Alvin Boyarsky and The Architectural Association).
27 SEI'CHI SHIRAI, *Noa Building*, Tokyo, 1973-5.
28 ARALDO COSSUTTA, *Crédit Lyonnais*, Lyon, 1975-6.

Late-Modern Slick-Tech and repetitive grid are used in this 900 foot tower to articulate the 'dumb box'. The top and bottom are exaggerated gestures; in scale with the whole tower but overpowering up close. The sense of massive impersonality is heightened by the ultra-smooth silver aluminium surface, the vast cantilevers at the base, the angular yet orthogonally disciplined volumes and the absolute geometry. All of this adds up to a consistent portrayal of the sublime, no doubt a welcome image for Citicorp. Certain oddities however lessen the impersonality: the horizontal layering versus vertical volume the raked top, sitting unevenly at 45°, waiting for its solar collectors (which will never be installed?) and the truncated pyramid lying on its side at the base, St. Peter's Church. The building mixes various functions – shopping center, offices restaurant, covered atrium as well as church – in a return to the grand New York tradition, celebrated by Rem Koolhaas in *Delirious New York* as the 'culture of congestion'. The metaphors share something with the Chrysler Building, particularly that of skyblender since the white-silver aluminium can merge imperceptibly with the clouds. All in all then a contradictory symbol appropriate to the opposite pressures on the tall building.

29, 30, 31 HUGH STUBBINS and ASSOCIATES, *Citicorp Center*, New York

Ultimate skyscrapers, linear buildings which present a flat edge to scrape the sky, were built in Chicago and New York at the turn of the century. Skeletal construction combined with the visual formula of the Renaissance palazzo produced these three masterpieces. The Manhatten Building (left) organised the 16 storey mass as a complex interaction of the column and palazzo. Two types of bay window make up an inverted T-shape which is played against the flat windows above and the adjacent Corinthian pilasters, giving a syncopated rhythm of bays: A, A, A, BBB, A, A, A. Vertically the column is given a triple crown or grand crescendo. Burnham and Root's Monadnock Building (right) is the ultimate heavyweight skyscraper, not only because of its 6 foot load-bearing brick piers, but more because of its visual density. After the bottom floor the corner curves in and then chamfers back and flares out to obtain both an Egyptian massiveness and hovering quality. This density is underscored by the planar walls and absence of ornament or even sills: windows seem to be cut into a sheer rock face, Mount Monadnock. The Flatiron Building, the tallest and 'most famous building in the world' (for seven years) is another heavyweight. In fact it led to the lightweight sky-scrapers of Ponti and Pei (46, 47). The triangular shape is a direct extrusion of the site, an economic necessity, to the height of 300 feet. It ends in a flourish of French caryatids. The middle is a palazzo with very subtle double bay rhythms (A, B, A, A, B, A, A, B, A) while the end elevation is a column with a quadruple base and triple capital. Visible here is the urban law that the column wants to become a wall, the wall a slab and the slab a sky city (although the last stage is not reached).

32 WILLIAM LE BARON JENNEY, *Manhattan Building*, Chicago, 1890-1 (Howard N. Kaplan).
33 BURNHAM & ROOT, *Monadnock Building*, 1892.
34 D.H. BURNHAM & CO, *Flatiron Building* (originally *Fuller*), New York, 1902

The most elegant skyscraper is Louis Sullivan's Wainwright Building in St. Louis, designed before he wrote his seminal text 'The Tall Office Building Artistically Considered' (see above page 14). Nevertheless it illustrates these later statements. It is a 10 storey palazzo designed once again as a column with a massive base in brown sandstone, a shaft in red brick and a capital in red terracotta – the different reds and brown harmonising to produce a massive, exuberant whole. Visual refinement to increase the feeling of height is everywhere: corner piers are large, seven foot vertical vectors, while the two and one half foot inner piers shoot up faster. Terracotta spandrels are recessed behind these slightly to diminish the horizontal plane. A string-course is broken just above the base and then at the top it is carried around to bring the eye to a natural fulfillment of movement. To emphasise that the eye always wants to travel to the top Sullivan has ornamented it with a deep cornice and floriated, intertwining tendrils that frame small windows. Oddly this great skyscraper is in fact a low, 10 storey palazzo with a U-shape plan enclosing a courtyard; it might thus be classed a tiny skycity, but this view of it is only visible from the air.

The slab with setbacks was one solution to the problem of too many skyscrapers crowding out the light and air at the bottom of cavernous streets. The New York city zoning code of 1916 demanded certain setbacks for a tall building which occupied an entire block. Hugh Ferris in the twenties represented the effects of this law in a series of ghost-like drawings showing the envelope to be a ziggurat-like structure which could shoot up to infinity in the middle of the block. (As long as this middle was confined to 25 per cent of the block it could go as high as structure allowed.) Raymond Hood, in the Daily News Building (a dry run for the Rockefeller Center, 72) turned the ziggurat into a short slab with setbacks. He accented the vertical lines in white brick, set them against a recessed pattern of red and black brick spandrels and 'corrected' the optical illusion of a flair at the top by trimming in the uppermost screens. The Senate House in London had no such zoning codes to contend with, but like many tall buildings became a ziggurat slab to mark an important urban axis. Its silver-grey masonry, centralising buttress and classical detail are reminiscent of World War I memorials. The effect of the zoning code in New York can be seen in the 'gold skyscraper', the Grolier Building and other setback slabs on 51st Street.

37 HOWELLS & HOOD, *Daily News Building*, New York, 1929-30.
38 CHARLES HOLDEN, *Senate House*, London, 1931-2.
39 *View down Lexington Avenue and 51st Street*, New York, photographed

Curtain walls and skycakes have a certain affinity for technical reasons, but are not inevitably connected. An ear[ly] curtain wall (a glass skin cantilevered from the structure an[d] hung like a curtain), on the Hallidie Building in San Francisco 1917 is hung away from the interior structure so that a two-wa[y] blue grid is set up, emphasising both horizontal and vertic[al] directions equally. This 'neutral grid' is then surmounted to[p] and bottom by cantilevered Gothic detail – a double base an[d] crown – in blue and gold, the colours of the client, th[e] University of California. More usual however is the horizontall[y] emphasised Lever House, New York, 1952 which set th[e] standard for fifties skyscrapers with its green and blue tinte[d] curtain wall and asymmetrical massing. Two slabs, on[e] horizontal above an open ground floor, the other vertical an[d] separated from the base, allow space to flow freely betwee[n] parts and interior and exterior. The skycake is a natural result o[f] brick firewalls above and below the floor lines. Other technic[al] necessities also lead to it such as the hung ceiling, the ai[r] conditioning, lighting equipment and window radiators. Th[e] skycake reaches a Slick-Tech culmination in Houston wher[e] Philip Johnson's Art Deco stripes of black spandrels and tinte[d] windows, all held in the same plane, climb and turn asymmetr[i]cally.

40 WILLIS POLK, *Hallidie Building*, San Francisco, 1917.
41 GORDON BUNSHAFT & SOM, *Lever House*, New York, 1952.
42 PHILIP JOHNSON & JOHN BURGEE, *Post Oak Central Building*

Classic slabs were worked out and built by Modern architects in the fifties with various solutions to the curtain wall. The Alcoa Building in Pittsburgh is, inevitably, a large-scale advertisement for aluminium with its thin-gauge panels (1/8 of an inch, and given triangular facets for strengthening). In the background to the photograph (left) can be seen a later advertisement for U.S Steel. The Alcoa Building is an early Slick-Tech solution with its rounded, green-tinted windows, its exterior panels sprayed in the inside for heat resistance, and its shimmering, light dissolving facets which break up the mass. Mies van der Rohe's Seagram Building, by contrast, is a 'heavyweight' solution to the glass curtain wall with its bronze I-Beams, dark spandrels and glass. This became the classic solution for offices but actually it was first worked out by Mies on an apartment building in 1951. The I-beams serve a decorative, non-structural purpose (although they stabilise window cleaning equipment) they give vertical accent and proportion to the mass. Both buildings keep a faint echo of the skycolumn in their under stated base and crown. Both led to the omnipresent 'dumb box and therefore a departure point for Late- and Post-Modernists

43 HARRISON & ABROMOWITZ, *Alcoa Building*, Pittsburgh, 1955.
44, 45 MIES VAN DER ROHE, *Seagram Building*, New York, 1958

Skyknife and skyberg, the broken side of a skyscraper, creates cutting edges in both cases. The angular profile, the razor seen slicing the sky, has been a metaphor and design motif at least since the Flatiron Building (34). Here and overleaf we see classic solutions to this metaphor. The Pirelli Building in Milan creates its drama by ellipsis, by leaving out material at a crucial juncture. The flat roof, a very thin lid, seems to hover with no visible support, just a black shadow line, while the two facades bend back towards each other and then leave a void which shoots to the top. Nervi's tapering piers and the flush-line treatment of the surface make it an oversize papercutter. The John Hancock Building in Copley Square, Boston, also breaks down the 60 storey mass, breaking up the regular volume – in this case a rhomboid. This can be seen in the plans (overleaf) and also in the various views of the reflective glass which again lessen the weight. A virtue of this glass wall is that it acts as a foil to the surrounding historic buildings, in particular Richardson's Trinity Church. The mirror plate also takes up and changes toward its surroundings like a chameleon. Contrast and changing reflection, these are the two rhetorical means it uses to acknowledge one of the key centres of Boston. The 7 storey base relates to the height of the adjacent Copley Plaza Hotel. The two broken edges hold the street lines, while the mass of the building inflects diagonally towards the all important plaza. A Late-Modern masterpiece which is unusually responsive to its urban context.

46 GIO PONTI with P.L. NERVI, *Pirelli Building*, Milan, 1961, (The Architectural Association)
47, 48 HENRY N. COBB with I.M. PEI & PARTNERS, *John Hancock Tower*, Boston, 1968-72, 73-6.
Overleaf
49, 50, 51, 52 HENRY N. COBB with I.M. PEI & PARTNERS, *John Hancock Tower*, Boston, 1968-72, 73-6. (Photograph 52 by Gorchev)

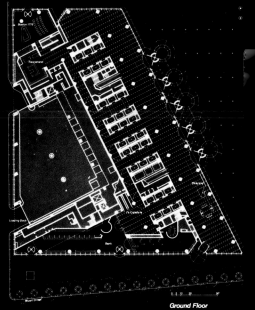

Ground Floor

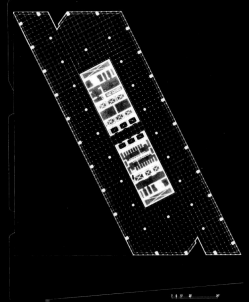

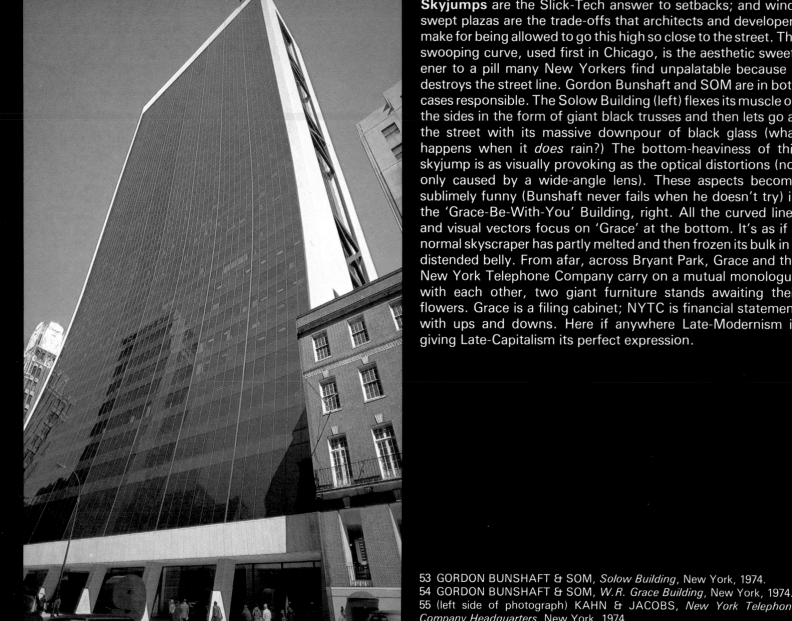

Skyjumps are the Slick-Tech answer to setbacks; and wind swept plazas are the trade-offs that architects and developer make for being allowed to go this high so close to the street. The swooping curve, used first in Chicago, is the aesthetic sweet ener to a pill many New Yorkers find unpalatable because i destroys the street line. Gordon Bunshaft and SOM are in both cases responsible. The Solow Building (left) flexes its muscle on the sides in the form of giant black trusses and then lets go a the street with its massive downpour of black glass (what happens when it *does* rain?) The bottom-heaviness of this skyjump is as visually provoking as the optical distortions (no only caused by a wide-angle lens). These aspects become sublimely funny (Bunshaft never fails when he doesn't try) in the 'Grace-Be-With-You' Building, right. All the curved line and visual vectors focus on 'Grace' at the bottom. It's as if normal skyscraper has partly melted and then frozen its bulk in distended belly. From afar, across Bryant Park, Grace and th New York Telephone Company carry on a mutual monologu with each other, two giant furniture stands awaiting thei flowers. Grace is a filing cabinet; NYTC is financial statemen with ups and downs. Here if anywhere Late-Modernism i giving Late-Capitalism its perfect expression.

53 GORDON BUNSHAFT & SOM, *Solow Building*, New York, 1974.
54 GORDON BUNSHAFT & SOM, *W.R. Grace Building*, New York, 1974.
55 (left side of photograph) KAHN & JACOBS, *New York Telephone Company Headquarters*, New York, 1974.

Shaped skyscrapers are a Late-Modern response to the rectangular box, and they may take their unusual shape for internal reasons of function, external reasons of site, or reasons best known to the designer. All are evident here. The Japanese pyramid (left) has large internal functions at the base, an auditorium for 2,400 and large entrance lobby. Above are conference halls, a traditional garden on the sixteenth floor, a hotel and restaurant near the top. This may explain its diminishing profile, but the peculiar handling of the two side walls and the entrance, which leans down like a xerox machine ready to disgorge copies, obviously have other motivations. In part they are the result of structural decisions. But clearly the idea of truncated pyramids leaning into each other was a motif that led to the form. The Vickers Tower responds, in its truncated curve, to a bend in the Thames River, and the path of the sun. The way this tower catches light and picks up the ripple of water, with its flashing silver mullions, is very pleasing. Both skyscrapers are, however, enigmatic in appearance since their distorted shapes seem to be responding to more particular determinants.

56, 57 NIKKEN SEKKI, *All Japan Working Youth's Hall*, Tokyo, 1973.
58 RONALD WARD & PARTNERS, *Vickers Tower*, London, 1963.

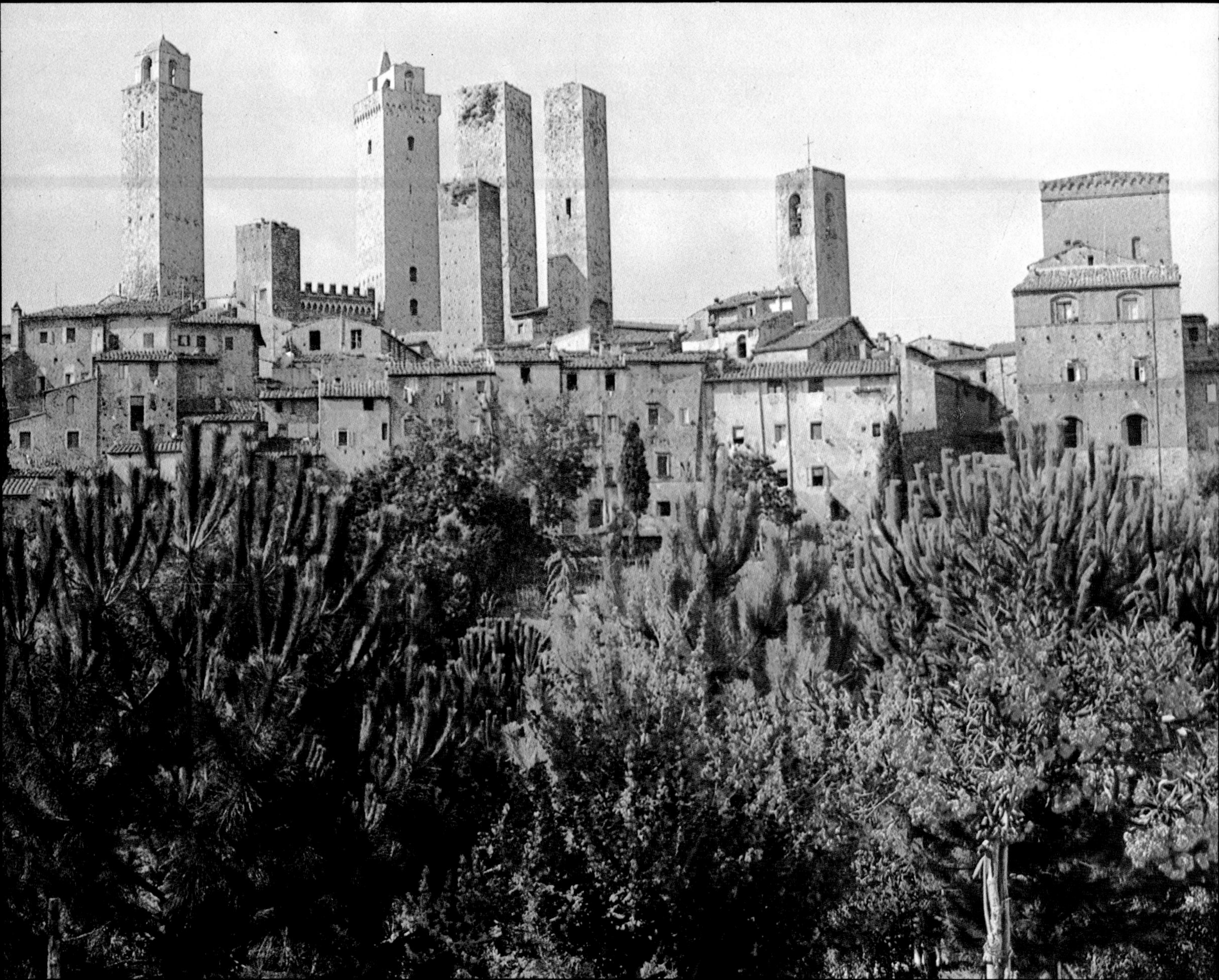

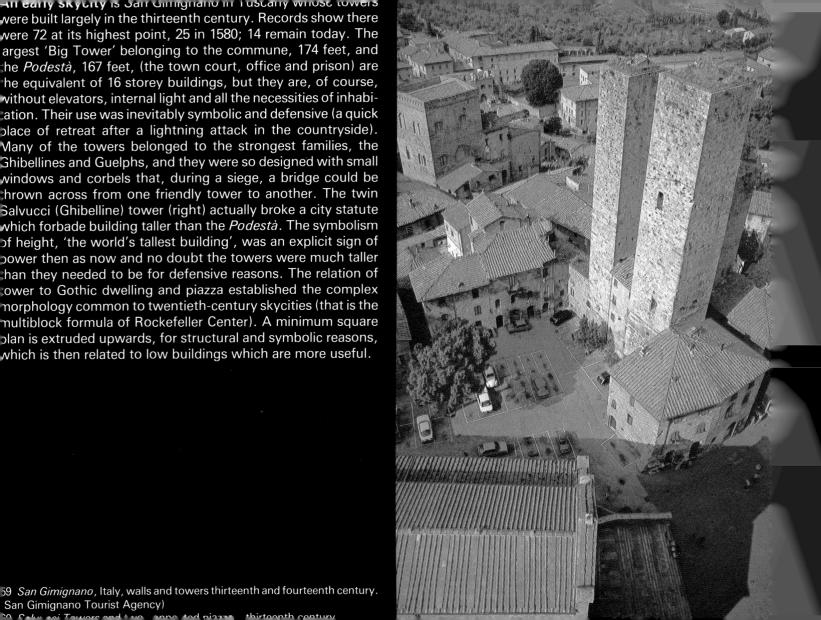

An early skycity is San Gimignano in Tuscany whose towers were built largely in the thirteenth century. Records show there were 72 at its highest point, 25 in 1580; 14 remain today. The largest 'Big Tower' belonging to the commune, 174 feet, and the *Podestà*, 167 feet, (the town court, office and prison) are the equivalent of 16 storey buildings, but they are, of course, without elevators, internal light and all the necessities of inhabitation. Their use was inevitably symbolic and defensive (a quick place of retreat after a lightning attack in the countryside). Many of the towers belonged to the strongest families, the Ghibellines and Guelphs, and they were so designed with small windows and corbels that, during a siege, a bridge could be thrown across from one friendly tower to another. The twin Salvucci (Ghibelline) tower (right) actually broke a city statute which forbade building taller than the *Podestà*. The symbolism of height, 'the world's tallest building', was an explicit sign of power then as now and no doubt the towers were much taller than they needed to be for defensive reasons. The relation of tower to Gothic dwelling and piazza established the complex morphology common to twentieth-century skycities (that is the multiblock formula of Rockefeller Center). A minimum square plan is extruded upwards, for structural and symbolic reasons, which is then related to low buildings which are more useful.

59 *San Gimignano*, Italy, walls and towers thirteenth and fourteenth century. (San Gimignano Tourist Agency)

60 *Salvucci Towers* and two connected piazza, thirteenth century

Delirious New York, the secret life of tall buildings, has finally been revealed in a book of that title by Rem Koolhaas. Through pseudo-psychoanalysis, and the paintings of his wife Madelon Vriesendorp (right) he uncovers the passions, betrayals and inner longings of these constructed people. Here Madame Chrysler is caught in the act with Monsieur Empire State by the flat-topped husband, (RCA, offstage in this painting) while the evidence, the spent Good Year Balloon, is there for all to see (the other skycharacters look in through the window). The two skyprickers are really 'landlocked lighthouses' whose beacons attract passing dirigibles (both had spotlights to shine on passing clouds and one was meant to be a mooring for blimps). The true confession of New York concerns the 'culture of congestion', the massive piling up of different functions and images in a compression of world history. All reality (or at least culture) is synthetically recreated here, put into one of 2,028 democratically equal blocks, and extruded upwards. Each block, according to the depth analysis, established its pre-existing 'mania', an urban fantasy. Hence the eclecticism of New York as a whole, hence the plurality of signs, the discontinuity of pure images, the personality and 'face' of each building. The actual view of New York (left) shows some of these giant people exchanging glances and leering, and the hybrid nature of each block, in itself often a skycity.

61 *View of Chrysler through the heads*, taken from West 40th Street.

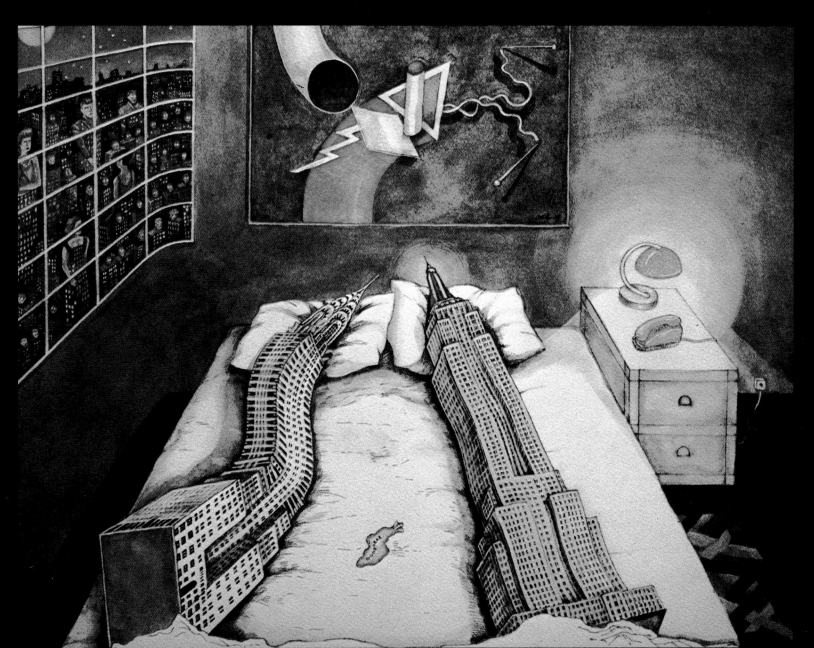

The urban law that a skypricker wants to become a sky, scraper which wants to become a skycity can be seen in the Metropolitan Life Insurance Company Building. The lower block was started in 1893 (and resurfaced in 1962) and the tower, a version of the Campanile in Venice (right) was built in 1909. This 700 foot tower was the 'World's Tallest Building' for four years until it was topped by the Woolworth Building (66). It is, like the San Gimignano tower, a square shape extruded vertically, and like the campanile, one capped with an ornament (clock), arcade, pyramid, lantern (to hold another lighthouse searchlight) and golden finial. Together this skypricker and skyscraper fill up a building lot, the one acting as maximum advertisement, the other as maximum rental. To its left can be seen Harvey Wiley Corbett's grand skylump, an even greater exploitation of real estate, with its deep plan and squat massing. The heaviness was decreased by the facets and setbacks according to Hugh Ferris' formula of the tall building as a pyramidal mountainscape. The Romanesque tower in the Piazza San Marco, rebuilt after a collapse in 1912, is more beautifully proportioned than its New York offspring. A brick shaft with shallow pilasters and no division into storeys (or large disturbing windows) leads the eye up to a triple crown with a nice syncopation of material. The arcaded bell-chamber surrounded by Istrian stone is a pleasing climax before the final, topmost ornament; the same rhythm was followed with Big Ben (7).

63 NAPOLEON LE BRUN & SONS, *Metropolitan Life Insurance Company Building*, New York, 1893, 1909, and left HARVEY WILEY CORBETT, *North Building*, 1932.
64 NAPOLEON LE BRUN & SONS, *Metropolitan Life Insurance Company Tower*, 1909.

metaphor for grand civic buildings and commercial ventures Cass Gilbert epitomised the 'cathedral of commerce' with hi Woolworth Gothic in 1913, the 'tallest building in the world' fc a short time, at 800 feet. A thirty storey Gothic tower sits on th extension of the site, a base of 27 storeys, and this 'mounte tower' houses 14,000 people, a prototype of later skycities Woodrow Wilson pressed a button and lit, in a divine act 80,000 cathedral bulbs. The Gothic, off-white terracotta cladding is given a classical bay rhythm ABBA, BB, BBB, BB ABBA and the central piers rise sheer to the top crown. Th Municipal Building (right) has a smaller tower mounted on U-shaped base. The facade holds the street line and embrace traffic (which used to flow through it). The wedding-cak profile with its temple top and gilded statue (to 'Civic Fame' was a prototype for Stalinist skycities and the Wrigley Building in Chicago (far right). This last building, a major urban monu ment in a part of Chicago which has one of the great collections of skycities, inflects towards the river to one side and plaz behind. Eclectic skycities tend to be flexible in their handling o urban space because of their compound shape: bending chopping and adding form is relatively easy. The Wrigley Building becomes a sparkling advertisement when its white gum-like surface is floodlit and the top searchlight is on. Again the clock has replaced the heraldic ornament, a fitting symbol tc the skycities' philosophy that 'time is money'.

66 CASS GILBERT, *Woolworth Building*, New York, 1913.
67 McKIM, MEAD & WHITE, *Municipal Building*, New York, 1914.
68 GRAHAM, ANDERSON, PROBST & WHITE, *Wrigley Building*, Chicago

Urban setpiece, one of the most successful groups of sky-buildings in the world, is in the Chicago loop area by the river. Five major eclectic landmarks can be seen and appreciated from a distance: the Chicago Tribune Tower (8, 9), the Wrigley Building (68) and the Carbide and Carbon Building, Stone Container Corporation and Lincoln Tower. Built during the twenties they carry on an urban discourse between 'mounted towers' and 'temples', Gothic fretwork and Corinthian columns. The result is an archetypal skycity. These buildings hold street lines and close axes with terminal ornaments. For instance, the Stone Container Corporation (left) curves inwards slightly to acknowledge the plaza formed by other buildings, and at the same time holds its tight, awkward site. A round 'Temple of Vesta' at the top focuses the eye in the middle of the building and gives it stability. Also it relates to similar caps which can be seen to left and right; notably the gold champagne crown on the 40 storey black granite and black terracotta Carbide and Carbon Building (related to Hood's Black Radiator Building, 11), and the radio-capped, mansard-Gothic of the Lincoln Tower. This last is a thin needle with the smallest floor space of any tall commercial building in Chicago.

69 ALFRED ALSCHULER, *Stone Container Corporation*, Chicago, 1923.
70 BURNHAM BROTHERS, *Carbide and Carbon Building*, Chicago, 1929.
71 HERBERT RIDDLE, *Lincoln Tower*, Chicago, 1928.

Grey skygraves, mute, heavy limestone slabs with their Art Deco gold trim and Beaux-Arts axes, mark the ultimate Capitalist skycity, Rockefeller Center in New York. A prototype for later downtown centers and 'comprehensive redevelopment', the great success of this one has led to the failure of so many others (except for the happy few, and the Portman developments). The mixture of building types (block, slab, sunken plaza), the mixture of functions (Radio City Music Hall, roof gardens, TV studios, offices, ice-skating rink in the focus, etc.) is unified by the similar formal treatment of stepped limestone slabs and grey aluminium. The ultimate view is down the 'English Channel' (left) with its gently pulling slope towards the ice-skating rink. The axis is reinforced by golden statues and the swooping edge of the RCA slab with its symmetrical setbacks. To the left is La Maison Française, to the right the British Empire Building and down below a changing sea of colourful flowers and bubbling water. The formal lessons of the Woolworth Building (66) by Cass Gilbert and the Daily News Building (37) by Raymond Hood (who was a key architect of this scheme) can be seen in the handling of the piers and setbacks. Interior murals and Art Deco symbolism, and exterior statues and decoration, celebrate the joys of work and capital in the social realist style of the thirties. Built and inhabited during this decade it was the greatest architectural attempt to end the depression.

72 REINHARD & HOFMEISTER; CORBETT, HARRISON & MACMURRAY; RAYMOND HOOD, GODLEY & FOUILHOUX, *Rockefeller Center*, New York, 1931-40.
73 *Rockefeller Center*, Lee Laurie *Atlas Sculpture*, 1933.
74 Relief and decoration on *La Maison Francaise*.

Twin tall buildings on a plaza have become a major type of skycity since the sixties with examples in many countries. The substitute of two 'dumb boxes' for one, the implication of a third (the space between), the introduction of a plaza are all expressive replacements for what has been taken away – a romantic profile, articulation of surface and content, eclectic style, base and capital. Semantically these boxes are 'all shaft'; technically they are skytubes with loadbearing structure in the walls (which results in small windows), and metaphorically they are legs or furniture pieces awaiting their bowl of flowers. The World Trade Center in New York shoots its aluminium Gothic 110 storeys to the sky, pointed arches below, anonymous *moiré* pattern in the middle and dainty filigree at the top. This was the 'world's tallest' for a *very* short time, for less than a year, and it got the Empire State Building so angry that it contemplated adding another 15 storeys to overshadow both the WTC and the Chicago Sears Building (82). The WTC has 10 million square feet of office space, seven times the Empire State Building, a Late-Capitalist accumulation which shows the development of more and more bulk towards less and less architectural interest. Yamasaki's twins at Century City in Los Angeles (right) are sparkling silver-grey triangles which also serve as urban navigation points. Their slick, blank Late-Modern surfaces also reflect long-term economic speculation and rental for a future (which hasn't yet arrived).

75 MINORU YAMASAKI ASSOCIATES and EMERY ROTH & SONS, *World Trade Center*, New York, 1962-77.
76 MINORU YAMASAKI ASSOCIATES, *Century City Towers*, Los Angeles, 1968-72.

Oxymoron is the rhetorical figure which makes these twin towers of Philip Johnson more interesting than others in the same genre. Visual paradox occurs at every angle. The buildings appear at first like the dark, simple boxes of Mies (45) with their regular I-beams and spandrels, but it is a 'complex simplicity' — a double whole, or one building split in two, implying a third trapezoid in the space between. The same surface appears to be different when seen from a different place because of the light angle. 'Opaque transparency' is the resultant paradox of this shifting view. The two black wedges, set very close on edge, cut a tall shimmer of light straight up for three hundred feet and, at the top, inflect towards each other creating an energy charge like two powerful electrodes. From within the atrium space walls seem to lean in and fall over the space frame roof, which sets up its own optical buzz, interference pattern and distortions. Reflections of one building on another, of passing clouds, dissolve the surface and give another oxymoronic contradiction, 'soft hardness'. This is a Late-Modern solution to the skycity which manages to give back to tall buildings the fantasy they had in the past. But it achieves this with the Minimalist means of the Slick-Tech aesthetic.

77, 78 PHILIP JOHNSON & JOHN BURGEE, *Penzoil Plaza*, Houston 1974-75.

Domesticated Piranesi is the theme of many Portman hotel interiors with their vast caverns of space shot through by dainty elevator cars decked out like gilded, Baroque pulpits. Here in the atrium space in Atlanta water surrounds the circular lily-pond seats in the cocktail lounge while circular white concrete masses push up through 5 storeys of green space and hanging vines. The circular elevator shaft bursts through the circular space frame and mounts outside for a view of the city. The base of this circular skycity holds a variety of functions, in a multi-block form, and this places it in the Rockefeller Center tradition, while the top has the inevitable restaurant and observation area. The contradiction between the ubiquitous circle and the rectangular, mirrorplate finish (a trademark of Portman hotels) is mildly interesting, but when one places these buildings in the great tradition of tall buildings – the Chrysler, the RCA – they are less forceful and imaginative than they seem at first.

79, 80 JOHN PORTMAN & ASSOCIATES, *Peachtree Center Plaza*, Atlanta, 1974-77.

Articulated skycities, versus the Minimalist geometrical sculpture, is a key opposition for current architects. Both examples and a mixture of the two can be seen here. José Louis Sert's Boston University Tower (far left) continues a tradition of articulation started by Le Corbusier and it makes distinctions visually between lecture halls, classrooms, elevator core, library (below) and pre-cast and in situ construction. These distinctions, proportioned by regulating lines Le Corbusier also used, produce a rich facade and vigorous modelling. The Sears Tower in Chicago (at 114 storeys the 'world's tallest' for ten years – a long reign in this business) is a Minimalist skycity with only technical articulations: the nine 'bundled tubes' are distinguished by the belted trusses every thirty floors and the elevator lines which run within each segment. Otherwise it is a black box with bright lights. The Tokyo Capsule Building has two Minimalist, black cores, bevelled at their top in the Japanese manner, which support 140 plug-in capsules. These are articulated one from another above a horizontal, concrete base. Here is the traditional tripartite organisation accompanied by material and constructional articulation: there is not, however, much distinction between functions.

81 SERT, JACKSON & GOURLEY, *Boston University Tower*, Boston, 1965.
82 BRUCE GRAHAM & SOM, *Sears Tower*, Chicago, 1968-70. (Hedrich-Blessing)
83 KISHO KUROKAWA & ASSOCIATES, *Nagakin Capsule Building*, Tokyo, 1971-2.

Skyberg and skyblob are the complicated and veiled fantasies latent in the Slick-Tech monoliths made from reflective glass. They revive the older traditions of romanticism, of escape from this earth which tall buildings allow. Here the fantasy is very much aided by the unearthly pile of silver glass, the 'greatest glass sculpture in the world' as one Texan put it, which again uses oxymoron, impossible contradictions, to great effect: the 'hard/softness' of the surface, the 'light/heaviness' of the mass, the 'black/whiteness' caused by sfumato and glistening reflections, the 'wet/dryness' also the result of Slick-Tech mirrorplate. The overall shape, seven setbacks which stagger up and down, curving at the head and ending in the long tail – the restaurant and observation tower – is very suggestive of animal forms. It also relates, perhaps unconsciously, to Art Deco furniture pieces of the thirties. The hotel is another in the John Portman genre, perhaps the most inventive and romantic: the inevitable atrium space climbs up in the middle between the side mirrorplate walls of bedrooms. The usual skyrestaurant is surrounded by Krypton bulbs which at night turn it into a full moon.

84, 85 WELTON BECKETT ASSOCIATES, *Reunion Hotel*, Dallas, 1976-77

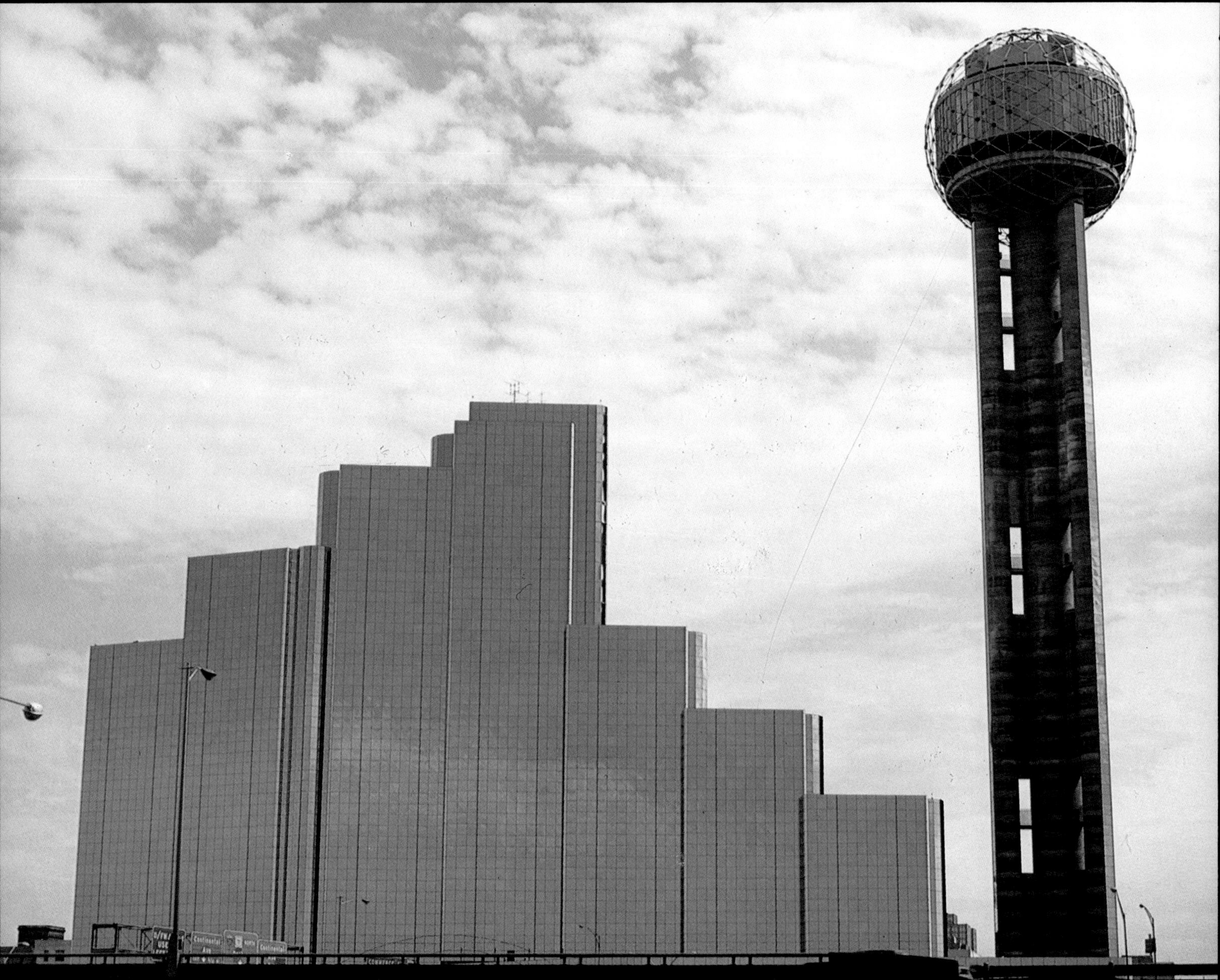
Continental
Ave
Continental

86 *Pittsburgh panorama*, photographed 1977.
87 *Hong Kong Bay*, Victoria, photographed 1979.

Skycities versus nature is an implicit theme of urban growth not only because they eat up space and pollute, but also because they create a second, artificial nature, a processed and invented copy of the landscape to be experienced in parks, gardens and parkways. The most felicitous contrasts occur when nature cannot be entirely obliterated, when there are physical limits as in New York City, Chicago, San Francisco (back cover) or here Pittsburgh and Hong Kong. The Golden Triangle in Pittsburgh is created by a curve in the river and a steep bluff beyond, both of which provide a dramatic contrast

to the high buildings. Visible here are remnants of the old city center, nineteenth-century towers dominated by the Alcoa Building and U.S. Steel. Hong Kong's old center is scarcely visible to the left of the tallest building, the Connaught Center. The future dominates, indeed dwarfs, the past. But the drama of man-made white slabs seen against the blue of the harbour and green of the mountains keeps the city impressive no matter what architectural assaults occur. The greater the buildings, the greater the contrast.

Notes

1 John Fleming, Hugh Honour & Nikolaus Pevsner, *The Penguin Dictionary of Architecture*, Harmondsworth, 1972, p.266.

2 Winston Wiseman, 'A New View of Skyscraper History', in *The Rise of an American Architecture*, edited by Edgar Kaufmann Jr., New York, 1970, pp.115-160.

3 Ibid., p.125.

4 Francisco Mujica, *History of the Skyscraper*, Archaeology and Architecture Press, New York, 1930, p.28.

5 Mark Mucasey, 'Morphology of the Skyscraper Office Building', paper written for my lecture course on Modern Movements, at the Architectural Association, 1977, p.30. This unpublished paper on which the author and I worked is a first approximation of the morphology used here, and it has proven very helpful in several respects.

6 *Chrysler Building 'The World's Tallest Building'*, compiled and published by John B. Reynolds, New York, 1930; kindly lent to me by Rem Koolhaas.

7 The point is that we all simplify when we classify according to the most pertinent feature, and this book is based on such simplifications; but we should still acknowledge the complexity.

8 Claude Bragdon, *The Frozen Fountain*, Alfred Knopfy, New York, 1932, p.11.

9 *Chrysler Building*, *op. cit.*, pp.15, 25, 7.

10 See Rem Koolhaas, *Delirious New York*, A Retroactive Manifesto for Manhattan, London and New York, 1978, p.108.

11 See Cervin Robinson and Rosemarie Haag Bletter, *Skyscraper Style* Art Deco in New York, Oxford University Press, New York, 1975, p.21; an excellent book on New York buildings of the twenties and their sources.

12 Wiseman, *op. cit.*, p.119.

13 An objection could be that one rarely sees the building from this position, and therefore that more pertinent metaphors are being suppressed. However, it *is* the privileged view – likely that of the designer who works on a model and plan drawings – and it is a conceptual one which is inferred as we walk through the tall building.

14 See Alan Balfour, *Rockefeller Center*, Architecture as Theatre, McGraw-Hill Inc., New York, 1978, p.38.

15 *Philip Johnson Writings*, edited by Robert Stern and Peter Eisenman, Oxford University Press, New York, 1979, p.265.

16 See Diana Agrest, 'Architectural Anagrams: The Symbolic Performance of Skyscrapers', *Oppositions II*, New York, Winter, 1977, pp.38, 43.

17 See Hugh Morrison, *Louis Sullivan, Prophet of Modern Architecture*, the Norton Library, New York, 1935, quoted from the 1962 edition, pp.148, 151.